THE
PIANO BE
OF
EASY CLASSICAL
MUSIC

Music Sales America

DISTRIBUTED BY

HAL•LEONARD®
CORPORATION

7777 W. BLUEMOUND RD. P.O. BOX 13819 MILWAUKEE, WI 53213

COVER PHOTOGRAPH BACKGROUND: SUPERSTOCK
EDITOR: AMY APPLEBY
EDITORIAL ASSISTANT: JACQUELINE TORRANCE

ORDER NO. AM 967549
US INTERNATIONAL STANDARD BOOK NUMBER: 0.8256.1824.X
UK INTERNATIONAL STANDARD BOOK NUMBER: 0.7119.8510.3

EXCLUSIVE DISTRIBUTORS:
MUSIC SALES CORPORATION
257 PARK AVENUE SOUTH, NEW YORK, NY 10010 USA
MUSIC SALES LIMITED
8/9 FRITH STREET, LONDON W1V 5TZ ENGLAND
MUSIC SALES PTY. LIMITED
120 ROTHSCHILD STREET, ROSEBERY, SYDNEY, NSW 2018, AUSTRALIA

PRINTED IN THE UNITED STATES OF AMERICA BY
VICKS LITHOGRAPH AND PRINTING CORPORATION

FOREWORD

FOR the pianist who loves classical music, the ideal piano bench should be sturdy, comfortable, and filled to the brim with rewarding masterpieces. The music books within should provide many pathways through the world of piano literature—and reflect a range of musical styles and moods.

This comprehensive volume provides the pianist with the ideal benchful of easy classical music. Here are the elegant preludes and dances of Purcell, Bach, and Handel; the favorite movements from piano concertos by Beethoven, Mozart, and Grieg; the exquisite nocturnes and waltzes of Brahms, Chopin, and Mendelssohn; the romantic short pieces of Schubert and Schumann; and the sublime impressionistic works of Debussy and Saint-Saëns.

The ideal piano bench should also include rewarding arrangements of great symphonic and chamber works. Within this volume, you will also find favorite selections from the concertos and suites of Bach, Scarlatti, and Vivaldi, as well as themes from the great orchestral works of Beethoven, Haydn, Rimsky-Korsakov, and Tchaikovsky. Great moments in opera and ballet are also provided in easy and rewarding piano arrangements, along with light classics by Waldteufel, Ivanovici, and Strauss. To double the fun, there's even a selection of easy, rewarding classical duets.

You hold in your hand enough easy classical piano music for countless hours of playing pleasure and musical discovery. In this piano bench, you are sure to find many of your dearest old friends, and perhaps a few new ones.

THE PIANO BENCH OF EASY CLASSICAL MUSIC

RENAISSANCE AND BAROQUE

CLASSICAL

ROMANTIC

IMPRESSIONIST AND MODERN

LIGHT CLASSICS

THEMES FROM THE OPERA

SCENES FROM THE BALLET

DUETS

Allegretto Scherzando

Carl Phillip Emanuel Bach
(1714–1788)

Moderately fast

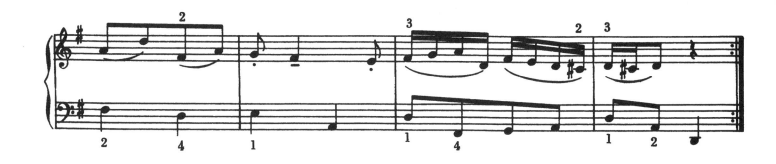

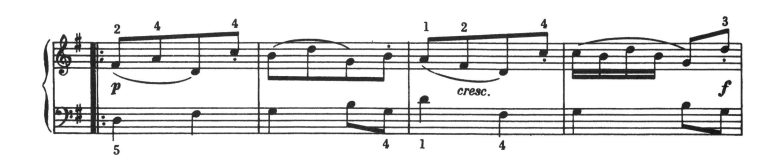

Prelude No. 2

from *Twelve Little Preludes*

Johann Sebastian Bach
(1685–1750)

STUDIO

Johann Christoph Friedrich Bach
(1732–1795)

Allegro

MINUET IN D MINOR

Johann Sebastian Bach
(1685–1750)

Slowly and calmly

Musette

Johann Sebastian Bach
(1685–1750)

Slowly and simply

March

from *The Little Notebook of Anna Magdalena Bach*

Johann Sebastian Bach
(1685–1750)

Allegro

Minuet in G

from *The Little Notebook of Anna Magdalena Bach*

Johann Sebastian Bach
(1685–1750)

Allegretto

Adagio

Ludwig van Beethoven
(1770–1827)

Smoothly

PARTITA No. 1

Minuet

Johann Sebastian Bach
(1685–1750)

Moderato

Prelude No. 9

Johann Sebastian Bach
(1685–1750)

Allegretto

SLEEPERS AWAKE

Andante

JESU, JOY OF MAN'S DESIRING

Johann Sebastian Bach
(1685–1750)

Simple and flowing

Air on the G String

Johann Sebastian Bach
(1685–1750)

Moderato

Gavotte

from *French Suite No. 5*

Johann Sebastian Bach
(1685–1750)

Moderato

RONDO

from *Orchestral Suite No. 2*

Johann Sebastian Bach
(1685–1750)

Moderato

BADINERIE

from *Orchestral Suite No. 2*

Johann Sebastian Bach
(1685–1750)

Allegro

Polonaise

Johann Sebastian Bach
(1685–1750)

Allegretto

Gavotte

from *Violin Sonata No. 6*

Johann Sebastian Bach
(1685–1750)

Andante grazioso

SHEEP MAY SAFELY GRAZE

from *Birthday Cantata*

Johann Sebastian Bach
(1685–1750)

Gently moving

Bourée

Johann Sebastian Bach
(1685–1750)

Air

Wilhelm Friedmann Bach
(1710–1784)

Moderato

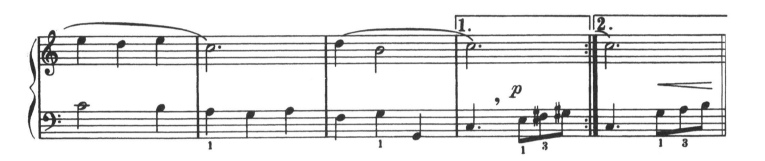

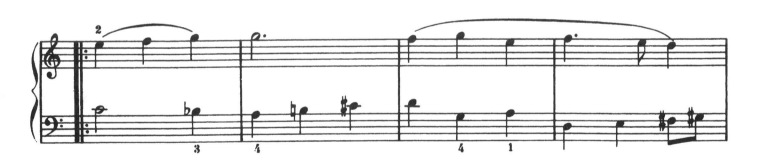

Minuet

Luigi Boccherini
(1743–1805)

Moderato

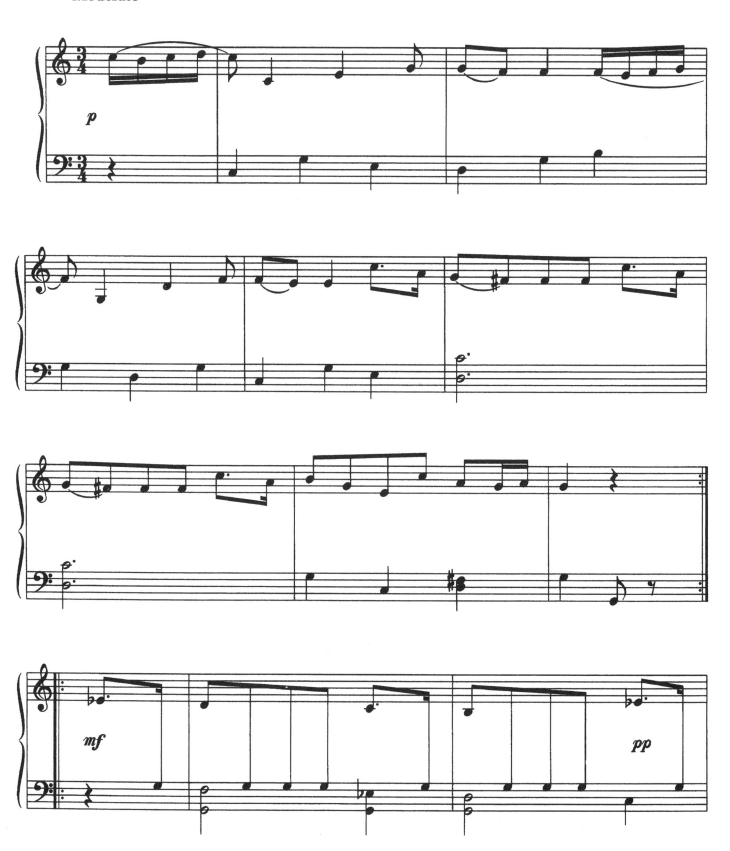

Fine

Gavotte in F

Arcangelo Corelli
(1653–1713)

Andantino

Tambourin

François Couperin
(1668–1733)

Allegro

Gavotte

George Frideric Handel
(1685–1759)

Andante

See the Conquering Hero Comes

from *Judas Maccabeus*

George Frideric Handel
(1685–1759)

Majestically

HALLELUJAH CHORUS

from *Messiah*

George Frideric Handel
(1685–1759)

Spiritoso

52

Bourée

George Frideric Handel
(1685–1759)

Animato

LARGHETTO

from *Concerto Grosso No. 12*

George Frideric Handel
(1685–1759)

Moderato

HORNPIPE

from *Water Music*

George Frideric Handel
(1685–1759)

Brightly

Air

from *Water Music*

George Frideric Handel
(1685–1759)

Andante

TRUMPET TUNE

Henry Purcell
(1659–1695)

With movement

Minuet

Henry Purcell
(1659–1695)

Andante

RIGAUDON

Jean-Philippe Rameau
(1683–1764)

Allegro

TAMBOURIN

Jean-Philippe Rameau
(1683–1764)

Allegro moderato

MINUET

Jean-Philippe Rameau
(1683–1764)

Moderato

Giga

Domenico Scarlatti
(1685–1757)

Allegro

* **Play as above**

****Begin trill on note above (A)**

Minuet

Domenico Scarlatti
(1685–1757)

Andantino

English Jig

Georg Philipp Telemann
(1681–1767)

Allegro

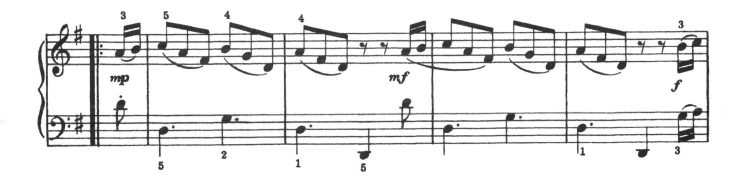

AUTUMN

from *The Four Seasons*

Antonio Vivaldi
(1678–1741)

Allegro

Minuet in G

Ludwig van Beethoven
(1770–1827)

Moderately

Für Elise

Ludwig van Beethoven
(1770–1827)

Poco moto

German Dance

Ludwig van Beethoven
(1770–1827)

Moderately

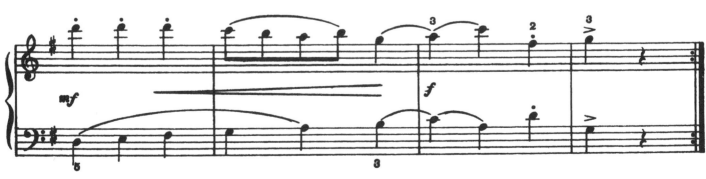

PIANO CONCERTO No. 3

First Movement

Ludwig van Beethoven
(1770–1827)

Lively

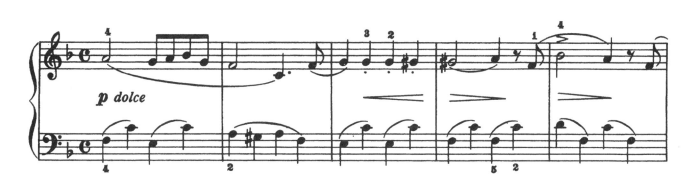

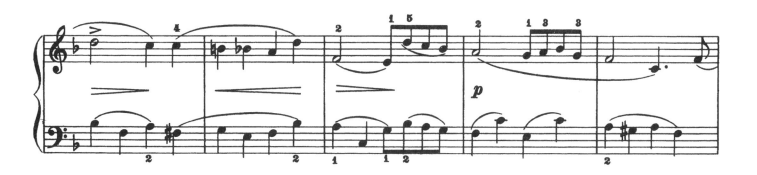

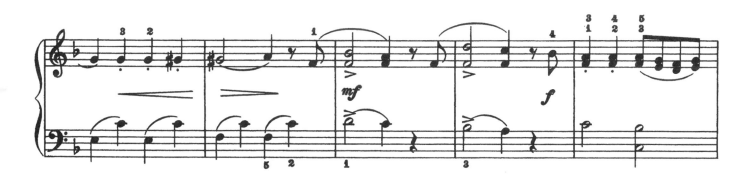

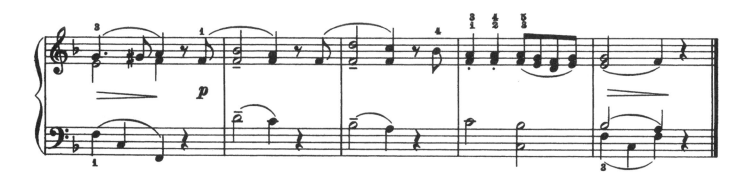

Piano Concerto No. 4

First Movement

Ludwig van Beethoven
(1770–1827)

Allegro moderato

legato

dim.

pp

MOONLIGHT SONATA

Adagio

Ludwig van Beethoven
(1770–1827)

Smoothly

SONATA IN G

Minuet

Ludwig van Beethoven
(1770–1827)

Moderato

Romance in F

Ludwig van Beethoven
(1770–1827)

Andante

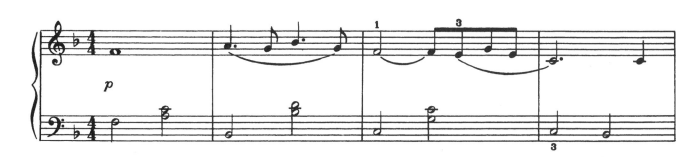

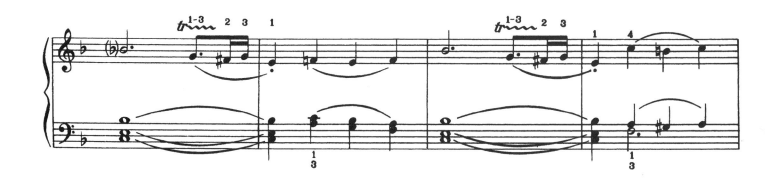

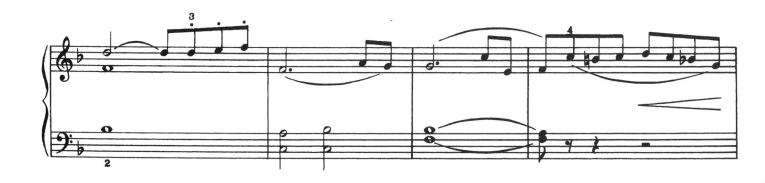

Pathétique Sonata
Second Movement

Ludwig van Beethoven
(1770–1827)

Adagio cantabile

con Ped.

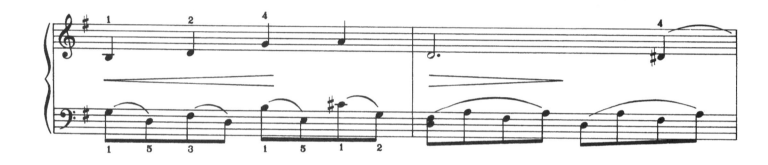

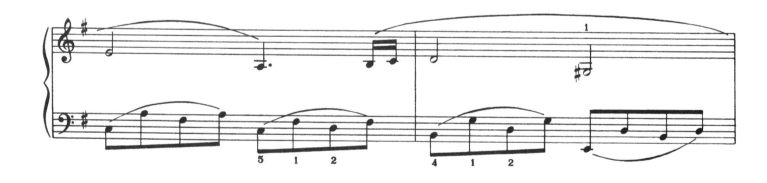

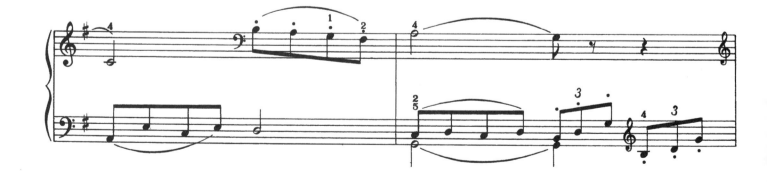

EMPEROR CONCERTO

First Movement

Ludwig van Beethoven
(1770–1827)

Allegro

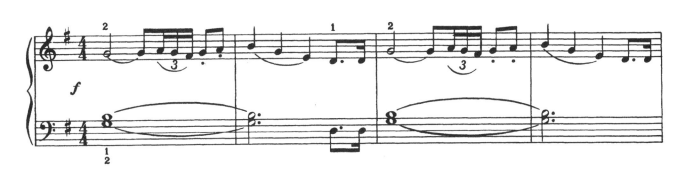

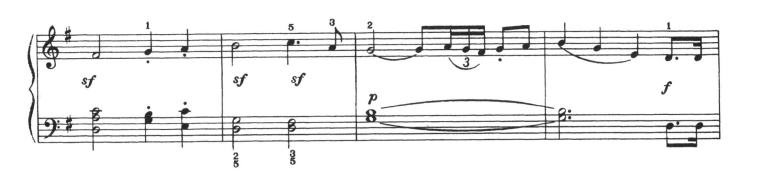

March

from *Egmont*

Ludwig van Beethoven
(1770–1827)

Vivace

Symphony No. 6

Canto Pastoral

Ludwig van Beethoven
(1770–1827)

Allegretto

Symphony No. 7
Second Movement

Ludwig van Beethoven
(1770–1827)

Allegretto

Symphony No. 9

Ode to Joy

Ludwig van Beethoven
(1770–1827)

Allegro

EROICA SYMPHONY

Theme

Ludwig van Beethoven
(1770–1827)

Allegretto

Rondino

Anton Diabelli
(1781–1858)

Allegretto

Walking

Anton Diabelli
(1781–1858)

Moderato

BAGATELLE

Anton Diabelli
(1781–1858)

Dance in G

Franz Joseph Haydn
(1732–1809)

Allegretto

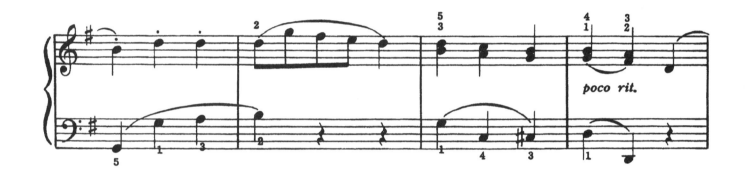

LITTLE GERMAN DANCE

Franz Joseph Haydn
(1732–1809)

Allegretto

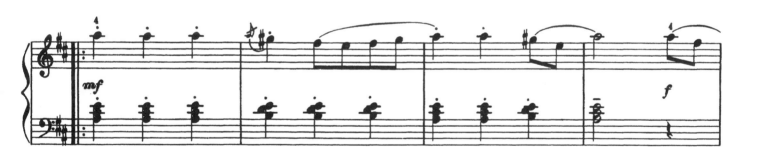

German Dance

Franz Joseph Haydn
(1732–1809)

Allegro con brio

D. C. al Fine

Minuet in B-Flat

Franz Joseph Haydn
(1732–1809)

Allegretto

(without pedal)

Fine

Trio

Symphony No. 97

Second Movement

Franz Joseph Haydn
(1732–1809)

Not too slow

Symphony No. 104
Second Movement

Franz Joseph Haydn
(1732–1809)

Moderato

TWO MINUETS
from *The Notebook for Nannerl*

Leopold Mozart
(1719–1787)

I

Allegretto

II

Andante

ARIETTA

Wolfgang Amadeus Mozart
(1756–1791)

Allegretto

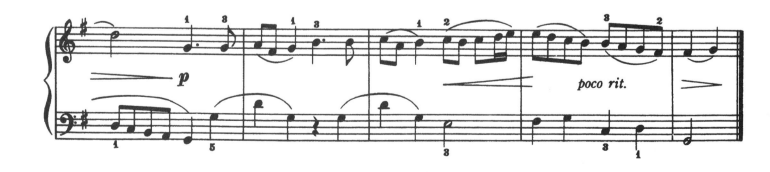

Air

Wolfgang Amadeus Mozart
(1756–1791)

Allegretto

Theme from Variations in A

Wolfgang Amadeus Mozart
(1756–1791)

Allegretto

Minuet in F

Wolfgang Amadeus Mozart
(1756–1791)

Lullaby

Wolfgang Amadeus Mozart
(1756–1791)

Moderately

Longing for Spring

Wolfgang Amadeus Mozart
(1756–1791)

Lightly

Minuet

Wolfgang Amadeus Mozart
(1756–1791)

Allegretto

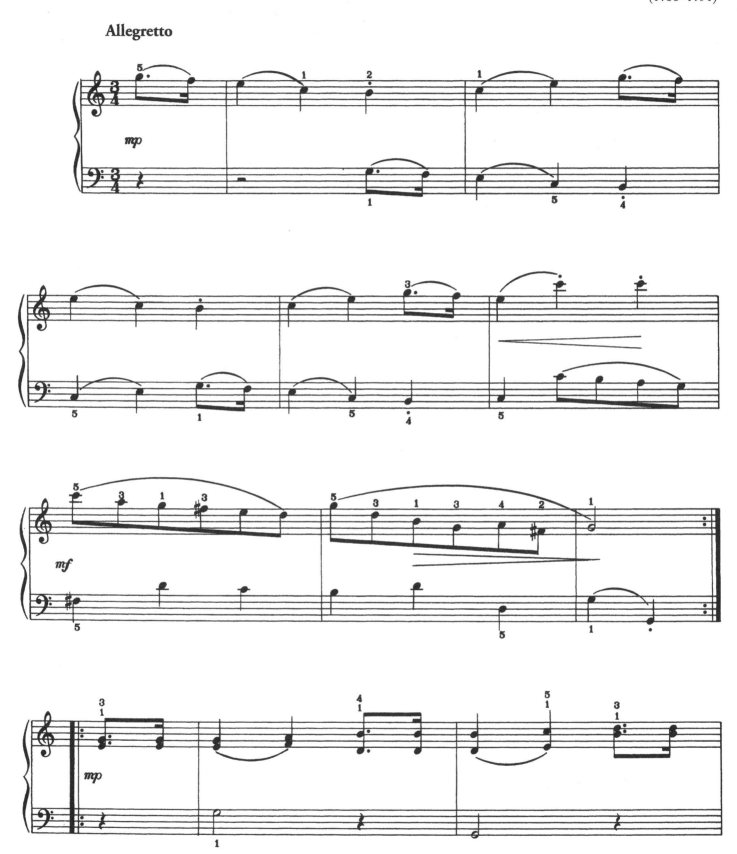

Sonata in A

First Movement

Wolfgang Amadeus Mozart
(1756–1791)

Andante grazioso

Piano Concerto in E-Flat

Slow Movement

Wolfgang Amadeus Mozart
(1756–1791)

Moderato

RONDO ALLA TURCA

Wolfgang Amadeus Mozart
(1756–1791)

Allegro

ROMANCE

from *Eine Kleine Nachtmusik*

Wolfgang Amadeus Mozart
(1756–1791)

RONDO

from *Eine Kleine Nachtmusik*

Wolfgang Amadeus Mozart
(1756–1791)

Allegro

Song to Friendship

Wolfgang Amadeus Mozart
(1756–1791)

A Musical Joke

Wolfgang Amadeus Mozart
(1756–1791)

Lively

Sonata for Violin and Piano

Last Movement

Wolfgang Amadeus Mozart
(1756–1791)

With movement

Piano Concerto No. 20

Wolfgang Amadeus Mozart
(1756–1791)

Andante

Piano Concerto No. 21

Wolfgang Amadeus Mozart
(1756–1791)

Andante

Sonata in C

Wolfgang Amadeus Mozart
(1756–1791)

Allegro

SINFONIA CONCERTANTE

Andante

Wolfgang Amadeus Mozart
(1756–1791)

Smoothly

SYMPHONY No. 40

Wolfgang Amadeus Mozart
(1756–1791)

Allegro

Jupiter Symphony

Minuet

Wolfgang Amadeus Mozart
(1756–1791)

Allegretto

The Cuckoo

August Eberhard Müller
(1767–1817)

Allegretto

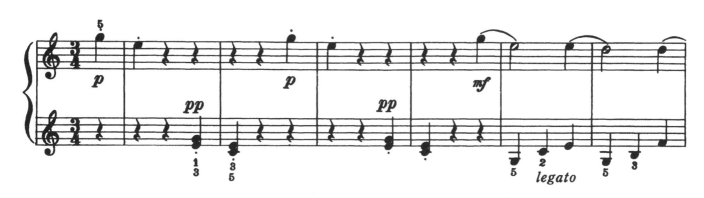

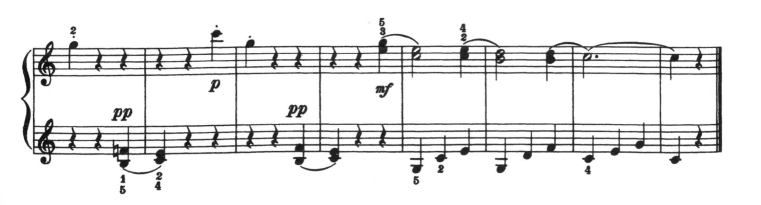

Waltz

Carl Maria von Weber
(1786–1826)

Allegro

Fine

Trio

f marc.

D.C. al Fine

Sonatina

Albert Biehl
(1835–1899)

Allegro moderato

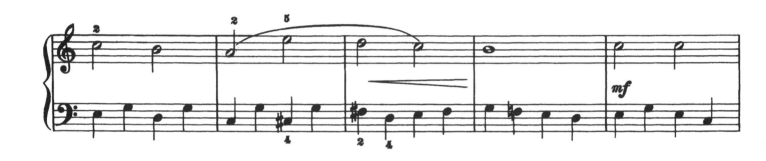

WALTZ

Johannes Brahms
(1833–1897)

Andante

Lullaby

Johannes Brahms
(1833–1897)

Andante

Symphony No. 1

Finale

Johannes Brahms
(1833–1897)

Moderate, steady motion

Symphony No. 3

Allegretto

Johannes Brahms
(1833–1897)

Smoothly

Hungarian Dance No. 6

Johannes Brahms
(1833–1897)

Allegro

Faster

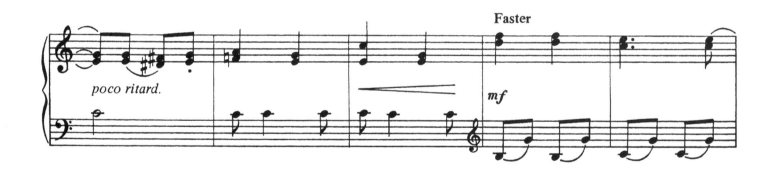

Hungarian Dance No. 4

Johannes Brahms
(1833–1897)

Fantasie-Impromptu

Frédéric Chopin
(1810–1849)

Waltz
Op. 34, No. 2

Frédéric Chopin
(1810–1849)

PRELUDE
Op. 28, No. 7

Frédéric Chopin
(1810–1849)

Moderato

Prelude
Op. 28, No.4

Frédéric Chopin
(1810–1849)

Largo

Nocturne

Frédéric Chopin
(1810–1849)

Moderato

Etude

Frédéric Chopin
(1810–1849)

Andante

Funeral March

Frédéric Chopin
(1810–1849)

Lento

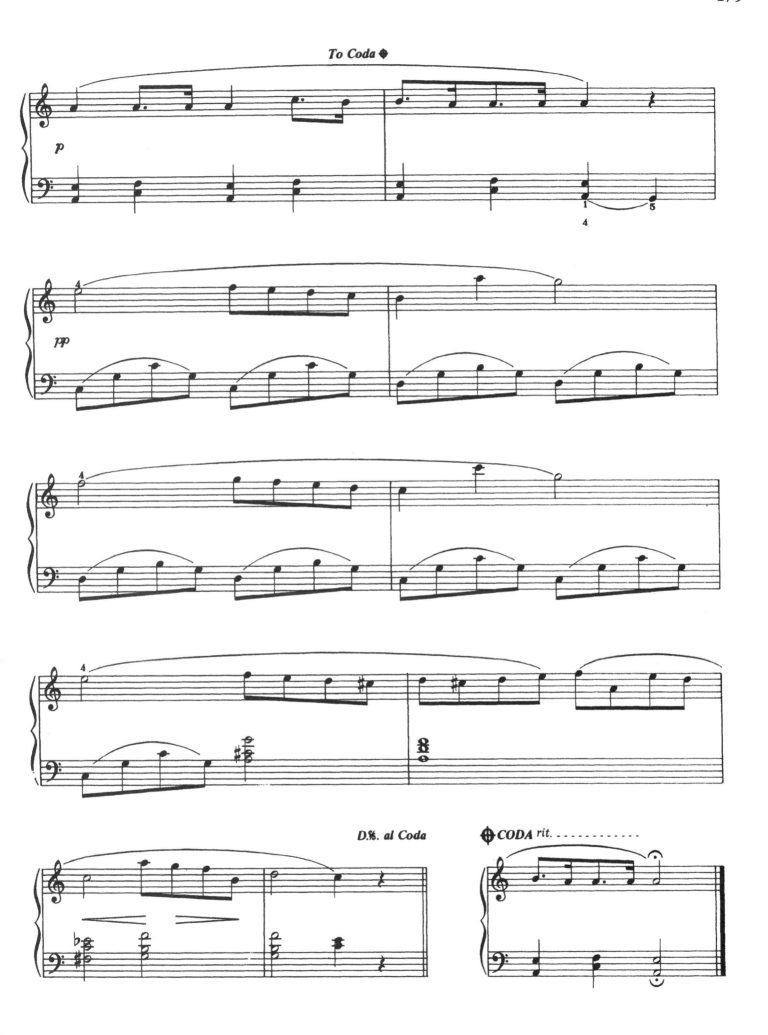

Mazurka

Frédéric Chopin
(1810–1849)

Allegro

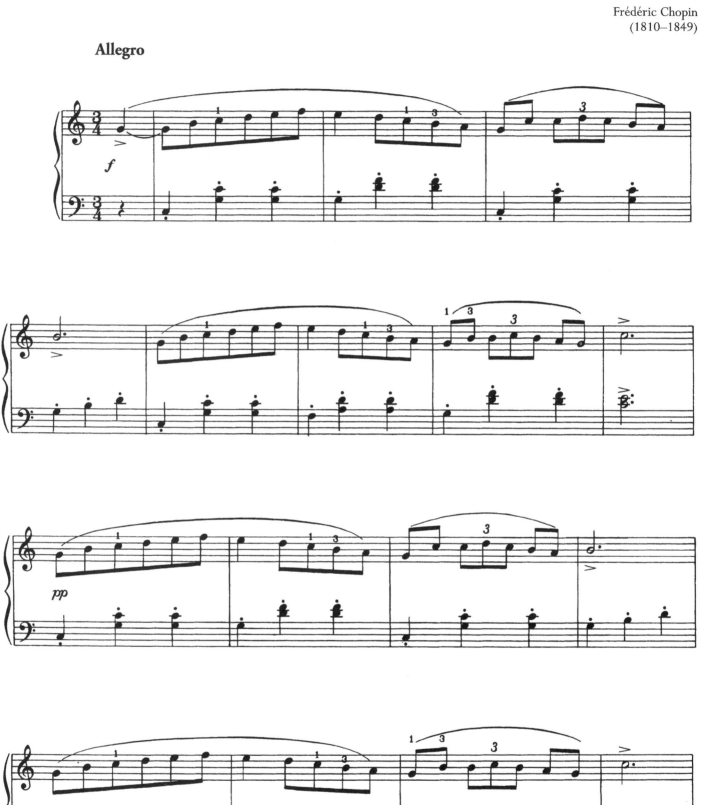

MILITARY POLONAISE

Frédéric Chopin
(1810–1849)

Allegro con brio

Piano Concerto

Theme No. 1

Edvard Grieg
(1843–1907)

Moderately fast

Piano Concerto
Theme No. 2

Edvard Grieg
(1843–1907)

I Love You

Edvard Grieg
(1843–1907)

Andante

Fingal's Cave

Felix Mendelssohn
(1809–1847)

Moderato

Liebestraum

Franz Liszt
(1811–1886)

Moderato

On Wings of Song

Felix Mendelssohn
(1809–1847)

Andante

NOCTURNE

from *A Midsummer Night's Dream*

Felix Mendelssohn
(1809–1847)

Andante tranquillo

O for the Wings of a Dove

Felix Mendelssohn
(1809–1847)

Moderato

Symphony No. 3

Third Movement

Felix Mendelssohn
(1809–1847)

Larghetto

Symphony No. 4

Third Movement

Felix Mendelssohn
(1809–1847)

Moderato con moto

Marche Militaire

Franz Schubert
(1797–1828)

Allegro moderato

IMPROMPTU

Franz Schubert
(1797–1828)

Allegretto

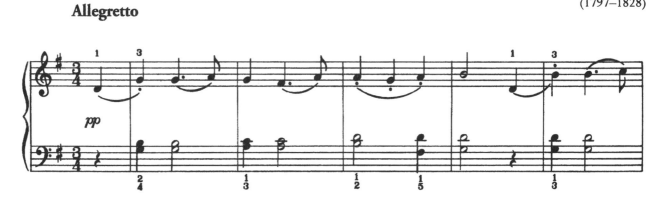

Who Is Sylvia?

Franz Schubert
(1797–1828)

Moderato

Ave Maria

Franz Schubert
(1797–1828)

Adagio

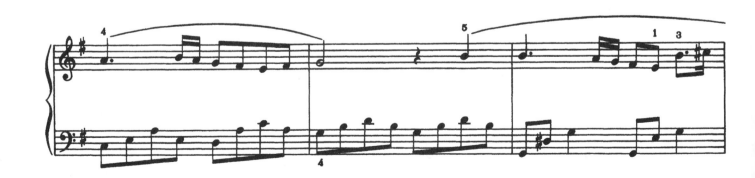

Death and the Maiden

Franz Schubert
(1797–1828)

Andante

Symphony No. 5

Second Movement

Franz Schubert
(1797–1828)

Moderato

Unfinished Symphony

Franz Schubert
(1797–1828)

Moderato

Chorale

Robert Schumann
(1810–1856)

Moderato

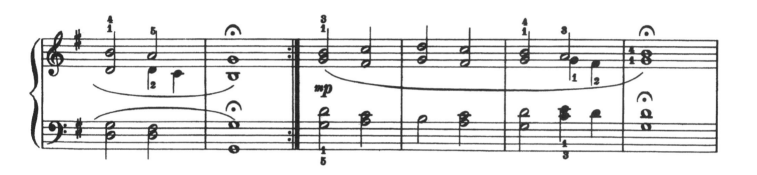

THE WILD HORSEMAN

Robert Schumann
(1810–1856)

Allegro con brio

Bagatelle

Robert Schumann
(1810–1856)

Moderato

SOLDIER'S MARCH

Robert Schumann
(1810–1856)

Allegro deciso

The Happy Farmer

Robert Schumann
(1810–1856)

Allegro animato

SLUMBER SONG

Robert Schumann
(1810–1856)

Allegretto

Andante Cantabile

Peter Ilyich Tchaikovsky
(1840–1893)

Andante

In a Little French Village

Peter Ilyich Tchaikovsky
(1840–1893)

With feeling

WALTZ

from *Serenade for Strings*

Peter Ilyich Tchaikovsky
(1840–1893)

Moderato

JUNE
Barcarolle

Peter Ilyich Tchaikovsky
(1840–1893)

Andante

Piano Concerto No. 1

Peter Ilyich Tchaikovsky
(1840–1893)

Majestically

Symphony No.5

Second Movement

Peter Ilyich Tchaikovsky
(1840–1893)

Andante

Pathétique Symphony

First Movement

Peter Ilyich Tchaikovsky
(1840–1893)

Andante

Clair de Lune

Claude Debussy
(1862–1918)

RÊVERIE

Claude Debussy
(1862–1918)

Andantino

Largo

from *New World Symphony*

Antonín Dvořák
(1841–1904)

Majestically

Slavonic Dance No. 10

Antonín Dvořák
(1841–1904)

Freely moving

Songs My Mother Taught Me

Antonín Dvořák
(1841–1904)

Andante

Poem

Zdeněk Fibich
(1850–1900)

Lento, with expression

with Pedal

To a Wild Rose

Edward MacDowell
(1860–1908)

Tenderly

Elegie

Jules Massenet
(1842–1912)

Lento, ma non troppo

with Pedal

The Young Prince and the Young Princess

from *Scheherezade*

Nikolai Rimsky-Korsakov
(1844–1908)

Andantino

HYMN TO THE SUN

Nikolai Rimsky-Korsakov
(1844–1908)

Andantino

Flight of the Bumble Bee

Nikolai Rimsky-Korsakov
(1844–1908)

Presto

ROMANCE

Anton Rubinstein
(1829–1894)

Moderato

Melody in F

Anton Rubinstein
(1829–1894)

Moderato

THE SWAN

from *Carnival of the Animals*

Camille Saint-Saëns
(1835–1921)

Adagio e legato

Farandole

from *L'Arlesienne Suite No. 2*

Georges Bizet
(1838–1875)

Allegro

POLKA

Mikhail Glinka
(1804–1857)

Allegretto

Danube Waves

Iosif Ivanovici
(c. 1845–1902)

Tempo di valse

Parade of the Wooden Soldiers

Leon Jessel
(1857–1942)

Gracefully

D.C. al Fine

Mattinata

Ruggiero Leoncavallo
(1857–1919)

Freely moving

Fascination

F.D. Marchetti

Waltz tempo

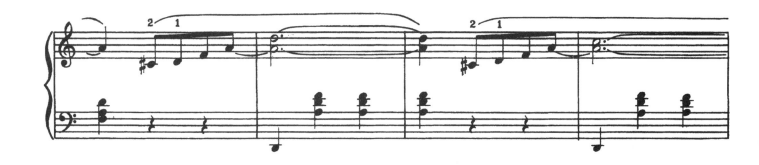

MIGHTY LAK' A ROSE

Ethelbert Nevin
(1862–1901)

Slowly and gently

Caprice No. 24

Niccolò Paganini
(1782–1840)

Brightly

THE WHISTLER AND HIS DOG

Arthur Pryor
(1870–1942)

OVER THE WAVES

Juventino Rosas
(1868–1894)

Valse moderato

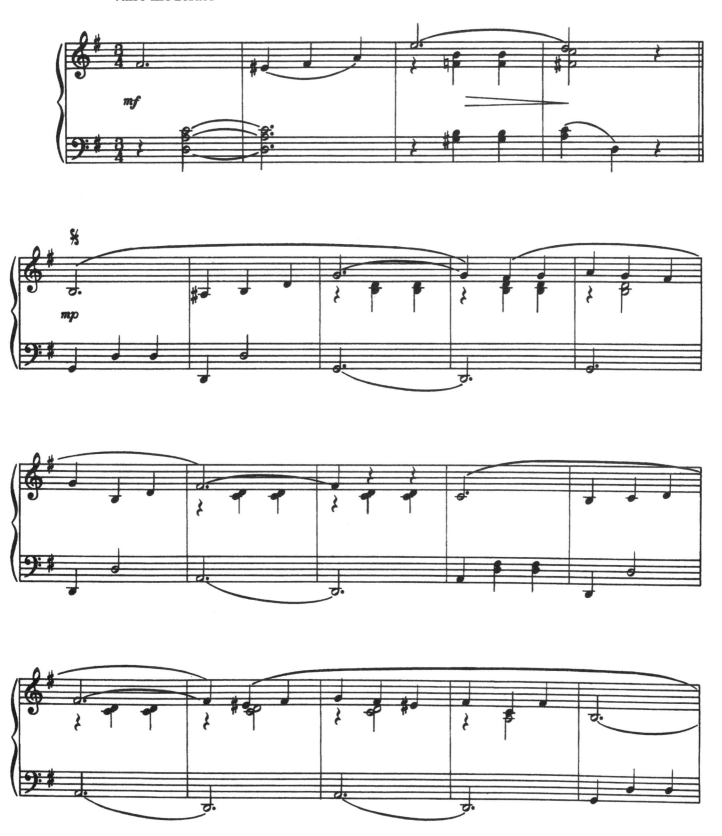

D. S. al fine

The Stars and Stripes Forever

John Philip Sousa
(1854–1932)

Moderato

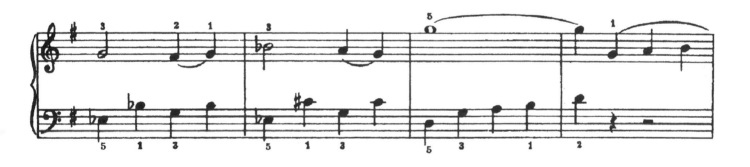

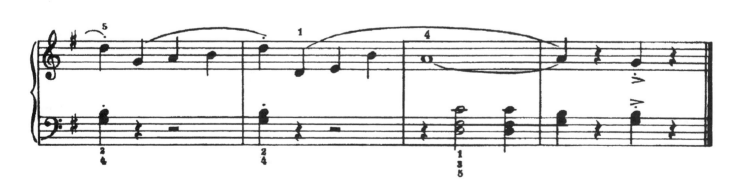

The Thunderer

John Phillip Sousa
(1854–1932)

Bright march

Tales from the Vienna Woods

Johann Strauss
(1825–1899)

Moderato

Blue Danube Waltz

Johann Strauss
(1825–1899)

Moderato

EMPEROR WALTZ

Johann Strauss
(1825–1899)

Valse Moderato

Estudiantina

Emil Waldteufel
(1837–1915)

Allegro

Goodbye

Francesco Paolo Tosti
(1846–1916)

El Choclo

A.G. Villoldo

Moderato

SKATERS WALTZ

Emil Waldteufel
(1837–1915)

Moderato

D.S. al fine

CASTANET SONG

from *Carmen*

Georges Bizet
(1838–1875)

Moderato

Habanera

from *Carmen*

Georges Bizet
(1838–1875)

Not too fast

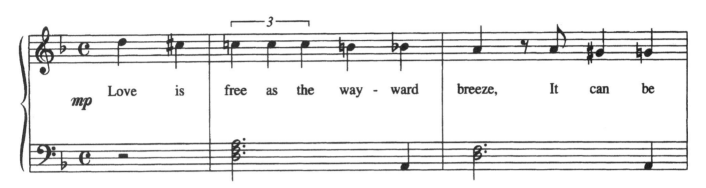

mp Love is free as the way - ward breeze, It can be

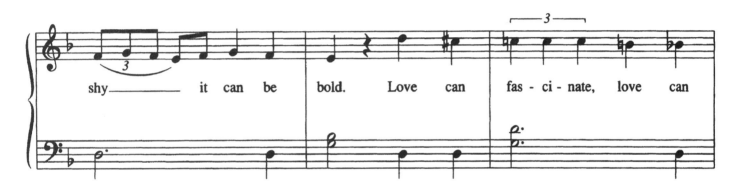

shy_____ it can be bold. Love can fas - ci - nate, love can

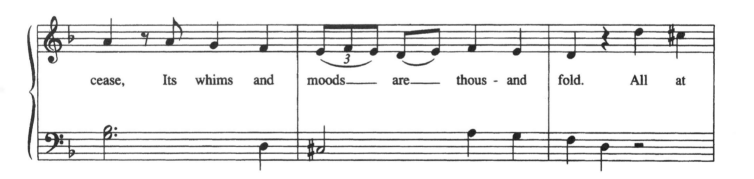

cease, Its whims and moods____ are____ thous - and fold. All at

once it ar - rives and ling - ers, For just how

Toreador's Song

from *Carmen*

Georges Bizet
(1838–1875)

Polovetzian Dance

from *Prince Igor*

Alexander Borodin
(1833–1887)

Moderato

THE BELL SONG

from *Lakmé*

Léo Delibes
(1836–1891)

Very lively

Ah! So Pure

from *Martha*

Friedrich von Flotow
(1812–1883)

Moderato

BERCEUSE

from *Jocelyn*

Benjamin Godard
(1849–1895)

Moderato

Oh! Wake not yet our dream, which guard-ian an-gels have at-tend-ed, And while the gold-en splen-dours gleam, Still sleep, my love, un-til 'tis

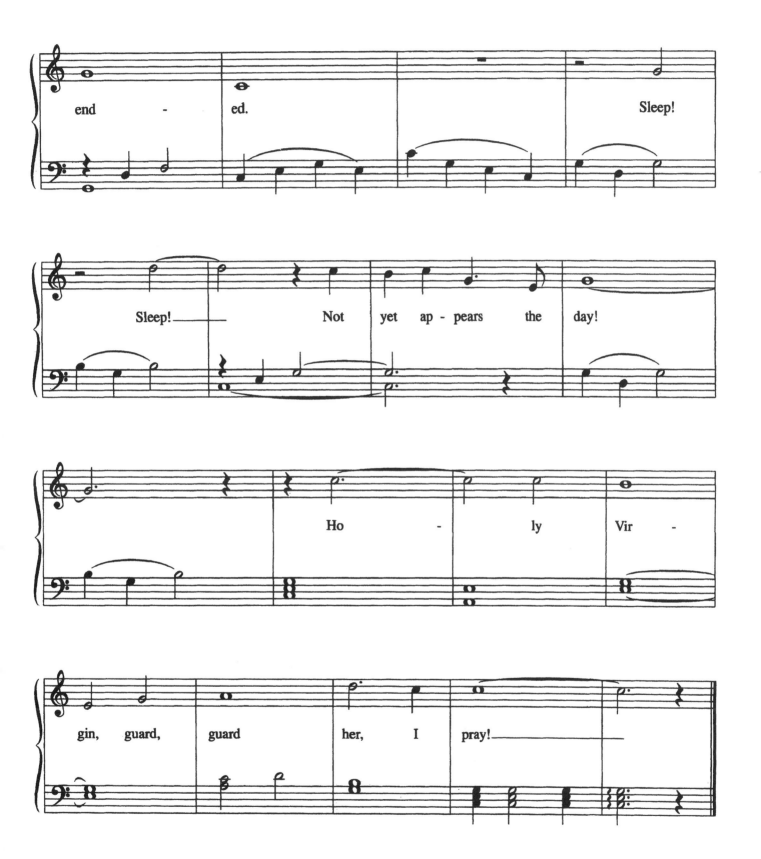

Waltz

from *Faust*

Charles Gounod
(1818–1893)

Moderato

sempre staccato

Morning

from *Peer Gynt*

Edvard Grieg
(1843–1907)

Moderately fast

Solveig's Song

from *Peer Gynt*

Edvard Grieg
(1843–1907)

Andante

Largo

from *Xerxes*

George Frideric Handel
(1685–1759)

Majestically

On with the Motley

from *I Pagliacci*

Ruggiero Leoncavallo
(1857–1919)

Slowly

On with the mot - ley, on your face put the pow - der;

The peo - ple pay you to fur - nish them with fun.

If Har - le - quin your Col - um - bine steals from you,

laugh out, Pag - liac - cio, and all will shout "well done!"

MEDITATION

from *Thais*

Jules Massenet
(1842–1912)

Andante

THE BIRDCATCHER'S SONG

from *The Magic Flute*

Wolfgang Amadeus Mozart
(1756–1791)

Pour, O Love, Sweet Consolation

from *The Marriage of Figaro*

Wolfgang Amadeus Mozart
(1756–1791)

Not too slow

mf Pour, O love,——— sweet con - so - la - tion

on my lone - ly, my bro - ken— heart.———

Give— me— back— his— lost af -

fec - tion, Or,— I beg— you— let me

die, or, I beg you, let me die. Bring me com-fort in my

suf-f'ring, hear my bro-ken heart-ed sigh!___ Give me back my lord and

hus-band, or, I beg___ you___ let me

die,___ or___ let me die. Give me back___ my lord and

hus-band, or, I beg___ you, let me die!

Zerlina's Song

from *Don Giovanni*

Wolfgang Amadeus Mozart
(1756–1791)

Moderato

Dance of the Hours

from *La Gioconda*

Amilcare Ponchielli
(1834–1886)

Moderato

O Isis and Osiris

from *The Magic Flute*

Wolfgang Amadeus Mozart
(1756–1791)

D.C. al fine

BARCAROLLE

from *Tales of Hoffman*

Jacques Offenbach
(1819–1880)

Tempo di valse

I Remember the Starlight

from *Tosca*

Giacomo Puccini
(1858–1924)

Slowly

I re-mem-ber the star-light

and the per-fume of ros-es

a gar-den gate that o-pened

a foot-step as soft as an an-gel's—

I felt her fra-grant pres-ence . . .

we were lost in each

ONE FINE DAY

from *Madame Butterfly*

Giacomo Puccini
(1858–1924)

WHEN I AM LAID IN EARTH

from *Dido and Aeneas*

Henry Purcell
(1659–1695)

With movement

When I am laid,—— am laid—————— in earth, may my

wrongs—— cre - ate No trou - ble, no trou - ble in thy breast.

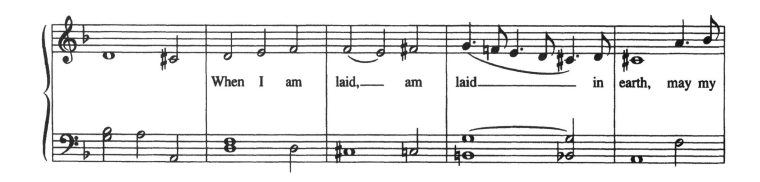

When I am laid,—— am laid—————— in earth, may my

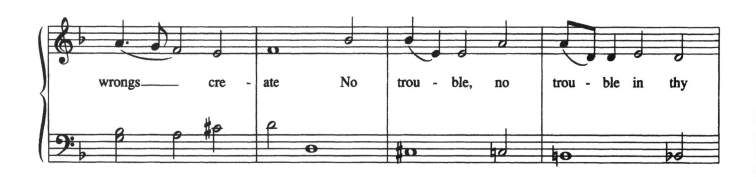

wrongs—— cre - ate No trou - ble, no trou - ble in thy

My Heart at Thy Sweet Voice

from *Samson and Delilah*

Camille Saint-Saëns
(1835–1921)

Larghetto

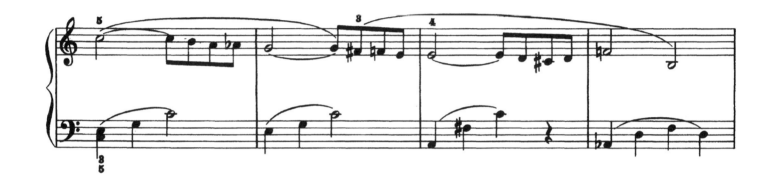

Caro Nome

from *Rigoletto*

Giuseppe Verdi
(1813–1901)

Moderately

You and You

from *Die Fledermaus*

Johann Strauss
(1825–1899)

Moderato

ANVIL CHORUS

from *Il Trovatore*

Giuseppe Verdi
(1813–1901)

Allegro

Woman Is Fickle

from *Rigoletto*

Giuseppe Verdi
(1813–1901)

Allegro

mf

Wo - man is fick - le and false al - to - geth - er,
Wret - ched the dupe is who when she looks kind - ly,

moved like the fea - ther borne by the bree - zes.
trusts to her blind - ly, this life is wast - ed.

Wo - man with smiles and with sighs can de - ceive us,
Yet he must sure - ly be all be - yond mea - sure,

of - ten can grieve us, ne - ver dis - pleas - es.
who of love's plea - sure ne - ver has tast - ed.

Evening Star

from *Tannhäuser*

Richard Wagner
(1813–1883)

Andante moderato

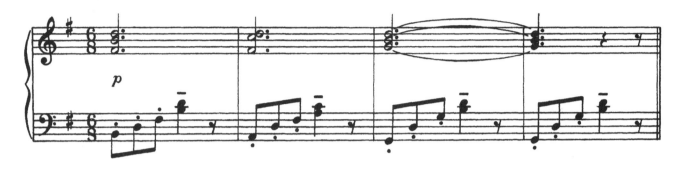

WALTZ

from *Coppélia*

Léo Delibes
(1836–1891)

Moderato

Pizzicato

from *Sylvia*

Léo Delibes
(1836–1891)

Allegretto

RONDEAU

from *Abdelazar*

Henry Purcell
(1659–1695)

Allegro animato

ENTR'ACTE

from *Rosamunde*

Franz Schubert
(1797–1828)

Andante

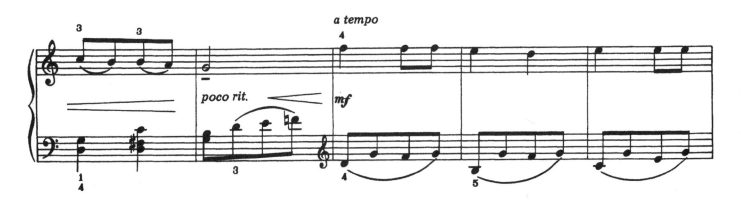

D.C. al Fine

WALTZ OF THE FLOWERS

from *The Nutcracker*

Peter Ilyich Tchaikovsky
(1840–1893)

Moderato

LOVE THEME

from *Romeo and Juliet*

Peter Ilyich Tchaikovsky
(1840–1893)

Andantino

WALTZ

from *Sleeping Beauty*

Peter Ilyich Tchaikovsky
(1840–1893)

Moderato

SCENE

from *Swan Lake*

Peter Ilyich Tchaikovsky
(1840–1893)

Moderato

Waltz

from *Swan Lake*

Peter Ilyich Tchaikovsky
(1840–1893)

Moderato

March

from *The Nutcracker*

Peter Ilyich Tchaikovsky
(1840–1893)

Moderato

Dance of the Sugar Plum Fairy

from *The Nutcracker*

Peter Ilyich Tchaikovsky
(1840–1893)

Andante non troppo

Symphony No. 1
Second Movement

Ludwig van Beethoven
(1770–1827)

Secondo

Andante cantabile con moto

Symphony No. 1

Second Movement

Ludwig van Beethoven
(1770–1827)

Primo

Andante cantabile con moto

Secondo

Primo

Hungarian Dance No. 5

Johannes Brahms
(1833–1897)

Secondo

Moderato

Hungarian Dance No. 5

Johannes Brahms
(1833–1897)

Primo

Moderato

Secondo

Primo

Surprise Symphony
Second Movement

Franz Joseph Haydn
(1732–1809)

Secondo

Andante

SURPRISE SYMPHONY
Second Movement

Franz Joseph Haydn
(1732–1809)

Primo

Andante

Musetta's Waltz

from *La Bohème*

Giacomo Puccini
(1858–1924)

Secondo

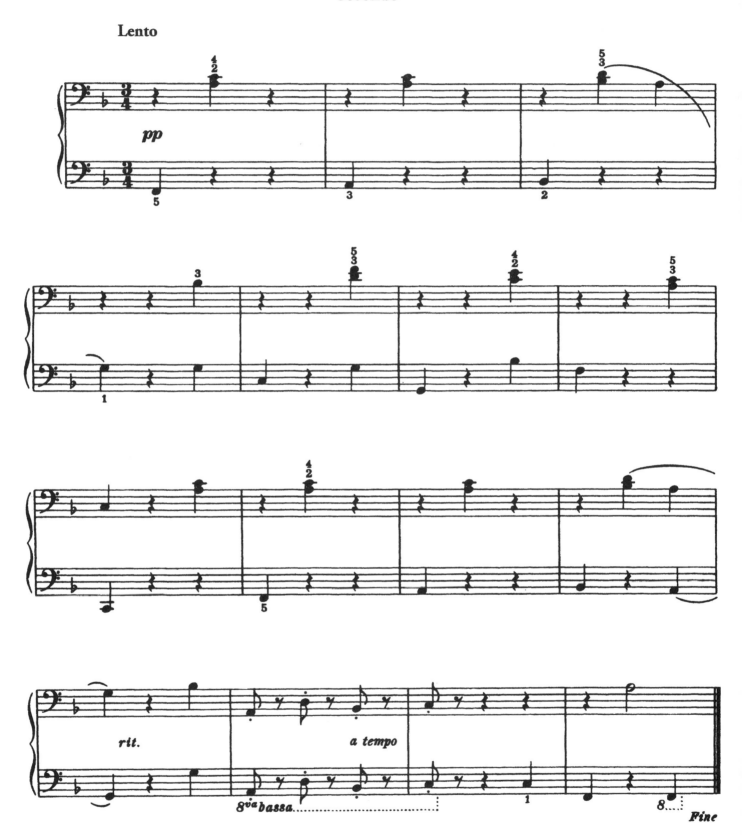

Musetta's Waltz

from *La Bohème*

Giacomo Puccini
(1858–1924)

Primo

Lento

Song of India

from *Sadko*

Nikolai Rimsky-Korsakov
(1844–1908)

Secondo

Andantino

Song of India

from *Sadko*

Nikolai Rimsky-Korsakov
(1844–1908)

Primo

Andantino

Secondo

Primo

Serenade

Franz Schubert
(1797–1828)

Secondo

Moderato

SERENADE

Franz Schubert
(1797–1828)

Primo

Secondo

Primo

Traumerei

Robert Schumann
(1810–1856)

Secondo

Moderato

Traumerei

Robert Schumann
(1810–1856)

Primo

Moderato

Pizzicato Polka

Johann Strauss (1825–1899)
and Josef Strauss (1827–1870)

Secondo

Moderato

Pizzicato Polka

Johann Strauss (1825–1899)
and Josef Strauss (1827–1870)

Primo

Moderato

Secondo

Primo

%al⊕Coda

Secondo

D.C. al 𝄋
e poi la Coda

⊕ Coda

Più Allegro

Primo

*D.C. al 𝄋
e poi la Coda*

Coda
Più Allegro

March Slav

Peter Ilyich Tchaikovsky
(1840–1893)

Secondo

Moderato

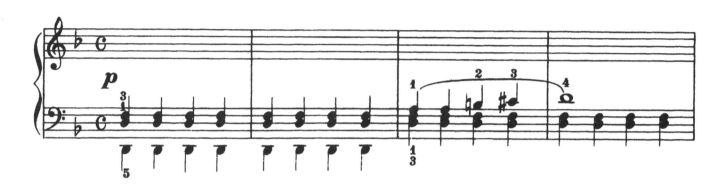